My Very First Bo[ok] to Make and Re[ad]

Little Books Designed as a First Reading Experience for Young Children

by

Kathy Dunlavy, Master Kindergarten Teacher
and
Jeri A. Carroll, Early Childhood Educator

illustrated by Tom Foster

Cover by Jeff Van Kanegan

Copyright © Good Apple, Inc., 1990

Good Apple, Inc.
1204 Buchanan St., Box 299
Carthage, IL 62321-0299

Copyright © Good Apple, Inc., 1990

ISBN No. 0-86653-557-8

Printing No. 98765432

Good Apple, Inc.
1204 Buchanan St., Box 299
Carthage, IL 62321-0299

Table of Contents

GA1163

GA1163

Introduction

My Very First Books to Make and Read is designed to meet the needs of young children as they encounter their first reading experience. The books use information that is relevant to young children and is current with their study and the time of year. The books allow the teacher to have a "reading" experience with a unit of study or theme that is normally presented to young children in preschool, kindergarten, first or second grade.

The idea for these books came home with Callie Carroll near Halloween after she had visited a Pumpkin Patch during *P* week in Kathy's kindergarten class at The Independent School in Wichita. Callie read her book to her mother in the car on the way home and was quite proud of her book and of her reading ability. That was only the first of many times her mother listened to that book.

GA1163

Each of the stories for the children is ready for them to make into a book which can be sent home with the children to read to their parents. One copy may remain in the reading corner for the children to read. Following the introduction and how to use these Little Books for Children is a section that shows possibilities and gives instructions for construction paper covers for these books.

Topics in this book are listed in order by month. At the end of the ten months there is a list of books that may be used any time throughout the year. There is a state book which may be used when you celebrate the birthday of your state. There is a birthday book that a child may make on the date of his/her birthday.

Books contain information about holidays, seasons, colors, shapes, sizes, numbers, thematic units, people, occupations, animals and about any other thing that is typically studied in the early years of school.

All of these books are based on vocabulary from the Dolch Word List, beginning readers, experiences that are common to the children and the typical phonics presented in kindergarten along with some concepts that are presented in early first grade.

Some of these books use a simple language pattern that is maintained throughout.

See the . . . .

A . . . can go.

Here comes . . . .

This is . . . .

Some of the books are simple one-word, one-picture books: circles, squares, rectangles, triangles, ovals

Some of the books give simple directions on how to do or make something:

Be My Valentine

Take some red paper. Fold it. Cut around your thumb.

Some use rhyming words:

The Magic Machine

Put in a hat. Out comes a cat!

Put in a log. Out comes a dog!

4

Some contain jokes:

X Ray

I see a leg bone.

I see an arm bone.

Is that a foot bone?

No! It is a dog bone!

All of the books contain sentences, ideas and magical thoughts appropriate for young children. They love to read them. They love to make them. They love to share them with their families and friends.

GA1163

How to Use the Books

It is suggested that these books not be used in isolation. They should not be cut out and presented to the children as *the* lesson on any one topic. They should follow a unit or concept of study. All of the books are written around topics that the young children have studied during their year in school . . . obviously not all in one year.

Step 1   Once the topic has been discussed, books can be presented to the children. Each child should get a copy of the two pages in this book that make the eight pages of his book.

Step 2   **Directions:**
The steps for constructing the book are on the last page of the children's book. The directions are almost the same in all of the books in order that the children will quickly learn to read the words. As they complete each step, they can check off each step. After they have done one or two books as a group, they should be able to make books on their own.

Step 3   **Read the story.**
Listen to the story.
Before making the two pages into a little book for the children to read, the teacher or children should read/listen to the story. The teacher should read the title and the first line of the story to the children. The concept and the language pattern should be apparent to the children as they hear that first line and look at that picture.

The teacher should ask for volunteers to read each of the next five lines. If there are no volunteers, the teacher should not hesitate, but go right ahead and read the lines until there are volunteers.

After the story has been read by various people, have the class read it together.

GA1163

Step 4   **Color the pictures.**
The next step for the children is to color the pictures which will give them one more chance to see/read the story as they color. Most of the pictures have been drawn in by an artist. Some leave space for the children to draw the pictures. If your children are older and can read well, you might want to white out the pictures before you copy them to test to see if the children can read for comprehension.

Step 5   **Cut out the pages.**
The children cut out the pages along the lines.

Step 6   **Put the pages in order.**
The children *put* the pages in order. (*Put* is a great Dolch word.)

Step 7   **Staple the pages.**
The children staple the pages together on the left-hand side of the title page to make the book.

Step 8   **Read the story.**
Children read their "books." They can read them to themselves, mumble read them, whisper read them or read them to friends.

Step 9   **Make a cover.**
Children can make covers for their books using paper and ideas suggested for the covers given in the next part of the book.

If your children are too young to follow the directions on how to make the books, you can make them up for your class. Read the story to the children one time and then place the book in your reading area for them to use. They will delight in reading the book to themselves or to their friends. Try placing the book in the housekeeping area and the children will play school or house and read to their children.

Making the Covers for the Books

If the children want, and you have the time, materials and patience, children can make special book covers for their books. We have given ideas for each of the books. Children will certainly come up with ideas of their own after you provide ideas for a few.

Book Covers for September

My School
Make an apple pattern. Place pattern of apple on piece of red construction paper on back of tablet. Use pin to "punch out" apple shape. Cut out. Glue apple onto right side of a folded 12″ × 6″ piece of construction paper. Add green leaf.

About Me
Have each child print his first name in black on the right side of a folded 12″ × 6″ piece of construction paper. Demonstrate how to make a star burst around his name using red, orange, yellow, green, blue and purple crayon.

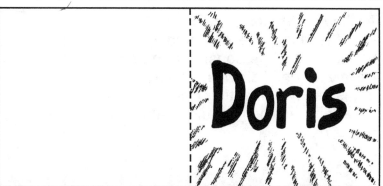

Stop and Go
Have each child cut out a red, yellow and green circle.
Glue them onto the right side of a folded 12″ × 6″ piece of black construction paper to resemble a traffic light.

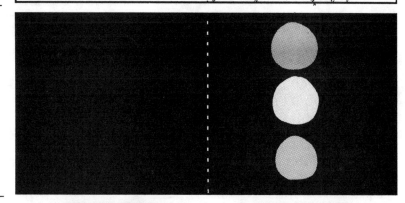

Safety
Have each child write the word *STOP* on the right side of the 12″ × 6″ folded piece of red construction paper. Cut off the corners of the book to make an octagon.

My Touch and Feel Book
Trace around the child's hand. Cut out the hand. Have children put on knuckles and fingernails. Glue hand onto the right side of a folded 12″ × 6″ piece of construction paper.

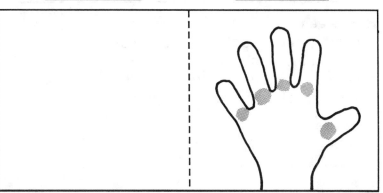

GA1163

Book Covers for October

Fall
Use sponge painting technique to paint fall tree on right side of a folded 12" × 6" piece of construction paper. Add brown painted trunk.

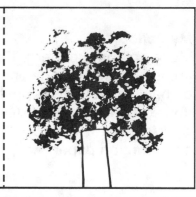

At the Fire Station
Use the right side of a folded 12" × 6" piece of white construction paper. Have each child draw or color a picture of his family's "meeting place" in case of a fire in their home. Label the picture.

X Ray
Discuss how an X-ray machine takes pictures of bones. Show actual X rays or human skeleton models. Let children cut bone shapes from 6" × 6" pieces of white paper. Glue onto the right side of a folded 12" × 6" piece of black paper.

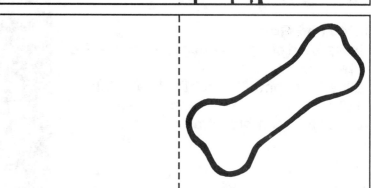

My Book of Shapes
Let children practice cutting circles, squares, triangles, rectangles and ovals. Glue the shapes in collage fashion on the right side of a folded 12" × 6" piece of paper.

Halloween
Pressing hard, color a Halloween scene on the right side of a folded 12" × 6" piece of white construction paper. Paint a black wash over the picture.

GA1163

Book Covers for November

Fruits

Have available magazines for children to cut out pictures of fruits. Glue onto right side of a folded 12″ × 6″ piece of construction paper.

Vegetables

Make a vegetable person using assorted colors of construction paper. Talk about possibilities—carrot arms, celery legs, tomato face, potato body, etc. Glue vegetable body parts on the right side of a folded 12″ × 6″ piece of black paper.

An Indian Story

Design an Indian blanket to be glued on the right side of a folded 12″ × 6″ piece of paper. Make heavy zigzag or wavy lines with black crayon. Fill in with heavy blue, red and orange. Feather ends of rectangle to resemble fringe.

Thanksgiving

Paint child's thumb red, palm brown and each finger a different color. Print on the right side of a folded 12″ × 6″ piece of blue paper.

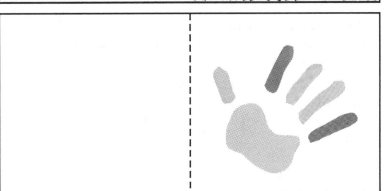

My Book of Colors

Give children a small coffee filter. Let them experiment with dabs of paint or food coloring on the filters. When the filter is dry, glue it on the right side of a folded 12″ × 6″ piece of paper.

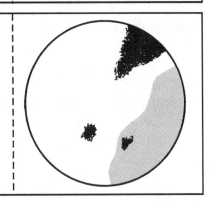

GA1163

Book Covers for December

My Teddy Bear
Children may design teddy bears from circles of brown felt paper to be glued on the right side of a folded 12″ × 6″ piece of paper. Decorate with buttons, fabric, etc.

Winter
Use coffee filters to make a snowflake. Glue it onto the right side of a folded 12″ × 6″ piece of blue paper.

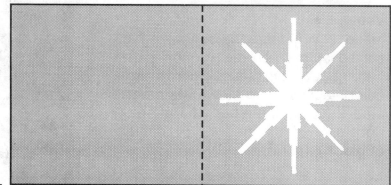

Bundle Up!
Using light-colored paper, trace around hand to make right and left mittens. Paint. Trim wrist with cotton. Glue one mitten on right side and one on left side of a folded 12″ × 6″ piece of paper.

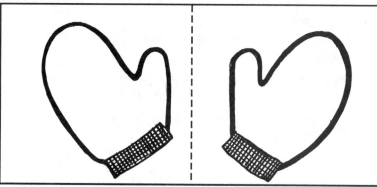

Christmas Is Coming!
Have each child cut a green triangle Christmas tree (and trunk). Decorate with beads, sequins, glitter, gummed stars, etc. Glue on right side of a folded 12″ × 6″ piece of white construction paper.

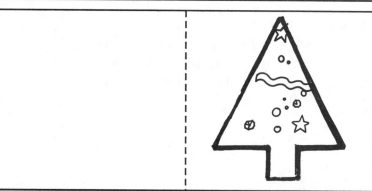

Under the Christmas Tree
Have Christmas stickers, ribbon and yarn available. Let children select a folded piece of 12″ × 6″ Christmas wrapping paper. Glue ribbon, stickers, etc., on right side of wrapping paper to resemble a gift.

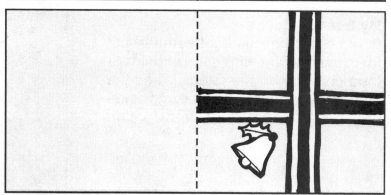

GA1163

Book Covers for January

The Thank-You Book
Design right side of a folded 12" × 6" piece of white paper to resemble an envelope. Use old stamps from home, school labels for return address and child's address for mailing address.

Potter Elemen
120 Euclid
North...

Tracks in the Snow
Provide an old pair of baby snow boots which can be dipped in white paint and pressed on brown paper. When dry, cut out and glue on right side of a folded 12" × 6" piece of paper.

A Bird Feeder
Design colorful winter birds. Have available bird pattern for tracing and cutting. Accent wing and tail with short rainbow-colored strips of tissue or construction paper. Glue on right side of a folded 12" × 6" piece of paper.

Let's Make a Snowman
Lay snowman stencil on right side of a folded 12" × 6" piece of blue paper. Use "snow" spray to create snowman. Remove stencil. Lightly spray remainder of cover.

Inventory
Supply children with simple graphs (5" × 5") that can be glued on right side of a folded 12" × 6" piece of paper. They may draw pictures in the first boxes of items they would like to inventory at home.

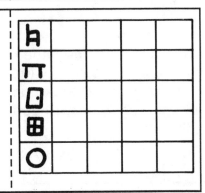

GA1163

Book Covers for February

Groundhog
Trace and cut two groundhogs—one on brown paper and one on black paper. Glue brown and black groundhogs on right side of a folded 12" × 6" piece of construction paper so that they resemble a groundhog and his shadow. Use crayons to add trees, grass, etc.

Be My Valentine
Follow the directions for making a valentine. Glue it onto the right side of a folded 12" × 6" piece of pink or white paper.

Photographs
Have each child color a self-portrait on a piece of white paper. Glue on the right side of a folded 12" × 6" piece of construction paper.

My Teeth
Cut a red oval to represent an open mouth. Glue small white rectangles to resemble upper teeth and lower teeth. Glue mouth onto right side of a folded 12" × 6" piece of construction paper.

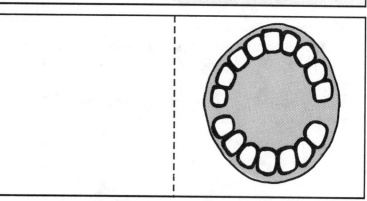

Hats
Make a funny hat for a book cover. Provide two Lincoln-shaped hat patterns, beads, silk flowers, yarn, ribbon, fabric, pipe cleaners, pom-poms, etc. Staple together with book in the middle.

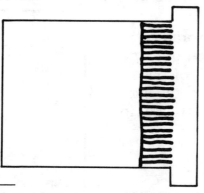
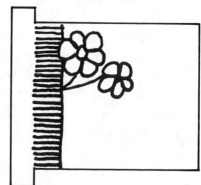

GA1163

Book Covers for March

Making a Pizza
Trace and cut 5" brown circle for pizza dough. Cut a smaller red circle with wavy edges for sauce. Use scraps to represent hamburger, pepperoni, mushrooms, green pepper, etc. Glue pizza on right side of a folded 12" × 6" piece of paper.

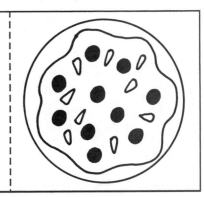

Making Things
Have available scraps of paper which can be cut into geometric shapes to make a sailboat, a robot, a truck, etc. Glue onto right side of a folded 12" × 6" piece of paper.

Show and Tell
Design a tote bag out of a folded 12" × 6" piece of construction paper. Staple strip of paper to front top and back top to resemble tote bag handles. Decorate front of tote bag with name or design. (Example: Jane's Bag)

The Circus
Design a clown face on the right side of a folded 12" × 6" piece of white paper. Use heavy black crayon to outine features of face in geometric shapes. Fill in with crayon.

Spring
Create a flower! Have assorted pastels and green paper available. Let each child cut and glue a spring flower onto right side of a folded 12" × 6" piece of light-blue paper.

GA1163

Book Covers for April

Easter

Cut 5″ egg shapes from white tag-board. Have children paint with pastel tempera paints. When dry, glue on right side of a folded 12″ × 6″ piece of paper (pastel color).

Rain

Trace and cut out umbrella. Glue on right side of a folded 12″ × 6″ piece of paper. Scatter dots of glue over page. They will resemble rain when glue dries.

Growing Plants

Provide paper in pastels and green. Have each child cut and glue parts of a plant (stem, leaf, flower) onto the right side of a folded 12″ × 6″ piece of paper. String or yarn may be used to represent roots.

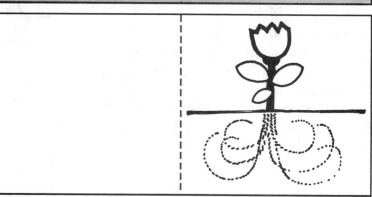

Birds

Cut bird patterns for children to trace onto the right side of a folded 12″ × 6″ piece of paper. Glue craft feathers onto the pattern and use moving eyes for the eye.

Going Camping

Create a sleeping bag. Fold a 5″ × 5″ piece of construction paper to resemble sleeping bag. A 5″ × 5″ piece of fabric can be glued to resemble lining. Fold down top of sleeping bag to expose a face peeping out. Glue onto the right side of a folded 12″ × 6″ piece of paper.

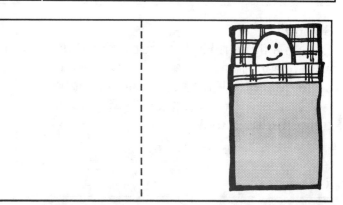

GA1163

Book Covers for May

A Nest

Have children shred brown grocery sacks into thin strips. Arrange strips in the shape of a bird nest and glue to the right side of a folded 12″ × 6″ piece of paper. Children may add bits of string, yarn, etc.

Ben Bug

Use directions from story to create a bug. Bug may be colored or made from paper scraps. Provide pipe cleaners for antennas. Glue or color on right side of a folded 12″ × 6″ piece of paper.

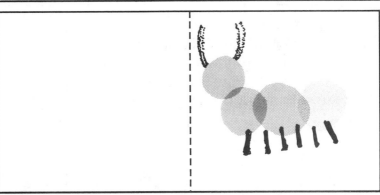

The Tall Book

Glue a pocket on the bottom of a 3″ × 12″ piece of paper. Give each child a 12″ tagboard strip to place in the pocket to measure things. Use a 3″ × 12″ piece for the back cover. Staple all together.

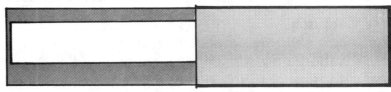

My Mom

Provide 7″ circles. Let each child decorate a face to look like his/her mom. Supply yarn, paper, crayons, markers, bangles, etc., to decorate. Glue onto the right side of a folded 12″ × 6″ piece of paper.

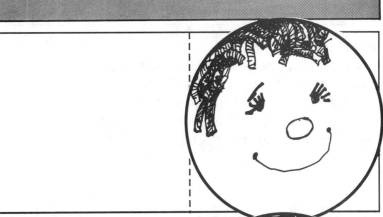

My Dad

Provide 7″ circles. Let each child decorate a face to look like his/her dad. Supply yarn, paper, crayons, markers to decorate. Glue onto the right side of a folded 12″ × 6″ piece of construction paper.

GA1163

Book Covers for June

Seasons

Provide pictures from old calendars. Let each child choose a picture that represents his favorite time of year. Trim the picture so it will fit onto the right side of a folded 12″ × 6″ piece of paper.

Fun in the Sun

Create a sand castle. Glue outline of sand castle on right side of a folded 12″ × 6″ piece of construction paper. Sprinkle with sand.

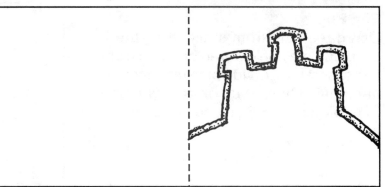

My Cat Book

Let each child use a stencil to trace a cat pattern on wallpaper. Cut out the cat and glue onto the right side of a folded 12″ × 6″ piece of paper.

Pet Parade

Provide crayons or magic markers. Let each child draw a picture of his pet on the right side of a folded 12″ × 6″ piece of paper. If the child does not have a pet, illustrate the classroom pet.

The Lost and Found Box

Have each child write the words *Lost and Found* on a 6″ × 6″ piece of brown cardboard. Use another piece for the back. Punch two holes on the left side. Tie loosely with yarn.

GA1163

Extra Book Covers

My Weather Book
Provide 5" paper plates, brad and a pointer. Attach to the right side of a folded 12" × 6" piece of paper. Use rulers to mark the circle into fourths. Illustrate sunny, rainy, cloudy and snowy in the quarters.

Rhymes
Provide a box of small pictures. Each child will choose one picture and glue it onto the right side of a folded 12" × 6" piece of paper. Child will think of and illustrate rhyming words.

I Have Feelings
Provide 7" circles for the children. Each may make a happy face for the front of his book and a sad face for the back using markers and crayons. Staple the sides and bottom of the face to resemble a pocket for the book.

My Book of Numbers
Children may cut numbers from the newspaper. (Sunday ads are especially good.) Glue the numbers in random style on the right side of a folded 12" × 6" piece of paper.

The Magic Machine
Challenge children to create the front of The Magic Machine on the right side of a folded 12" × 6" piece of aluminum foil. Provide collage materials for decorating.

GA1163

Extra Book Covers

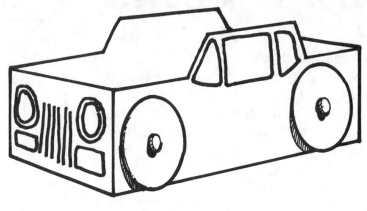

Things That Go
Provide construction paper. Let each child design a vehicle that can be glued to the side of a Velveeta or similar box. Provide brads for movable wheels. The Things That Go book can be placed in the box.

Dinosaur Story
Provide dinosaur stencils for crayon rubbings. Rubbing should be completed on the right side of a folded 12" × 6" piece of paper. The effect is one of fossil rubbings.

My State Book
Provide brochures or magazines featuring your state. Let each child cut out pictures and glue in collage fashion on a piece of paper the shape of your state. Provide a second for the back. Staple. Label.

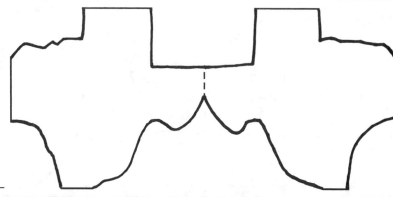

My Birthday Book
Provide balloon stickers. Let children count balloon stickers to correspond with their age. Arrange balloons on the right side of a folded 12" × 6" piece of paper. Embellish cover with confetti.

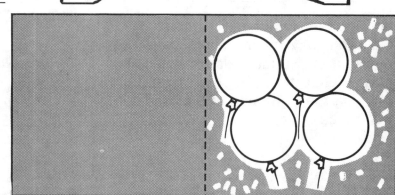

The Colors of the Rainbow
Use watercolor paints to paint rainbow on right side of a folded 12" × 6" piece of white construction paper.

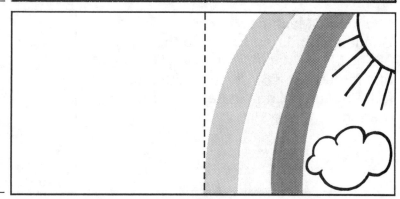

GA1163

1

This is my school.

2

This is my teacher.

3

This is my desk.

4

21

These are my friends.

5

This is my favorite thing.

6

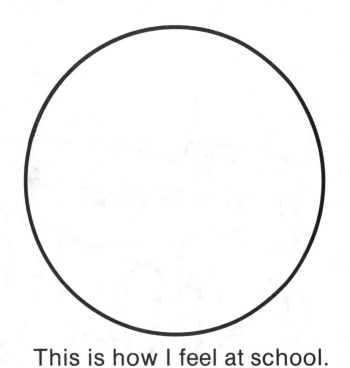

This is how I feel at school.

7

Directions:
1. Listen to the story.
2. Color the pictures.
3. Cut out the pages.
4. Put the pages in order.
5. Staple the pages.
6. Read the story.
7. Make a cover.

8

GA1163

1

Tom   Jill

Pam

Bob   Pat
        Ann

My name is _____.

2

I am _____ years old.

3

My address is

_____.

4

GA1163

My telephone number

is _____.

5

My hair is _____.

My eyes are _____.

6

I am _____ inches tall.

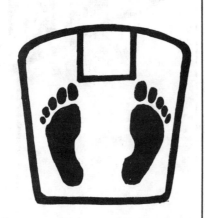

I weigh _____ pounds.

7

Directions:
1. Listen to the story.
2. Fill in the blanks.
3. Color the pictures.
4. Cut out the pages.
5. Put the pages in order.
6. Staple the pages.
7. Read the story.
8. Make a cover.

8

24

GA1163

STOP AND GO

1

Big cars go down the street.

2

Little cars go down the street.

3

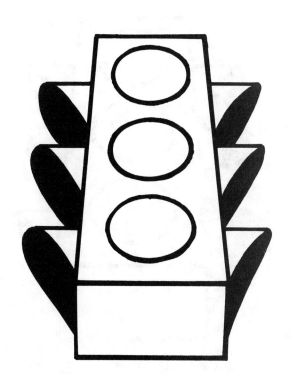

See the traffic light.

4

25

It is red. Stop!

5

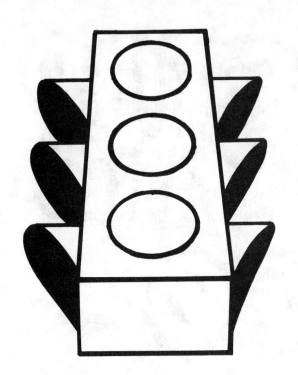

It is green. Go!

6

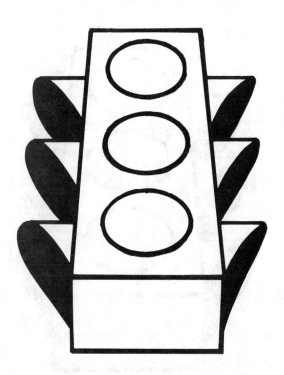

It is yellow! Be careful.

7

Directions:
1. Listen to the story.
2. Color the pictures.
3. Cut out the pages.
4. Put the pages in order.
5. Staple the pages.
6. Read the story.
7. Make a cover.

8

GA1163

SAFETY

1

2

WALK

3

DON'T
WALK

4

GA1163

Railroad

5

Telephone

6

School Crossing

7

Directions:
1. Listen to the story.
2. Color the pictures.
3. Cut out the pages.
4. Put the pages in order.
5. Staple the pages.
6. Read the story.
7. Make a cover.

8

GA1163

1

This is soft.

2

This is hard.

3

This is rough.

4

GA1163

This is smooth.

5

This is sharp.

6

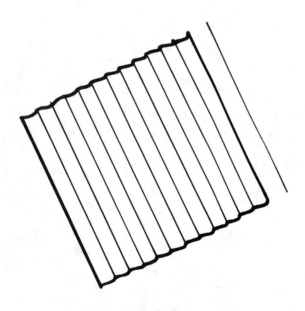

This is bumpy.

7

Directions:
1. Listen to the story.
2. Glue on the objects.
3. Cut out the pages.
4. Put the pages in order.
5. Staple the pages.
6. Read the story.
7. Make a cover.

Objects to use: cotton balls, flat buttons, sandpaper, satin fabric, toothpicks, corrugated paper.

8

GA1163

1

The days are cool.

2

Leaves fall down,

down,

down.

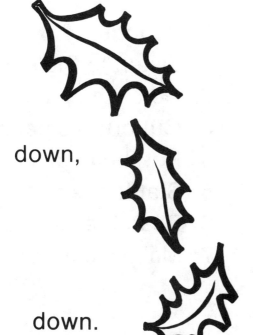

3

Apples are red and yellow.

4

31

Birds are flying south.

5

Children go back to school.

6

Animals get ready for winter.

7

Directions:
1. Listen to the story.
2. Color the pictures.
3. Cut out the pages.
4. Put the pages in order.
5. Staple the pages.
6. Read the story.
7. Make a cover.

8

GA1163

AT THE FIRE STATION

Here we are at the fire station.

2

1

We see the big red fire trucks.

3

We put on the fireman's hat and boots.

4

33

We learn about

STOP,

DROP

and ROLL.

5

We practice
STAY LOW AND GO!

6

The fireman helps you and me.

7

Directions:
1. Listen to the story.
2. Color the pictures.
3. Cut out the pages.
4. Put the pages in order.
5. Staple the pages.
6. Read the story.
7. Make a cover.

8

34

1

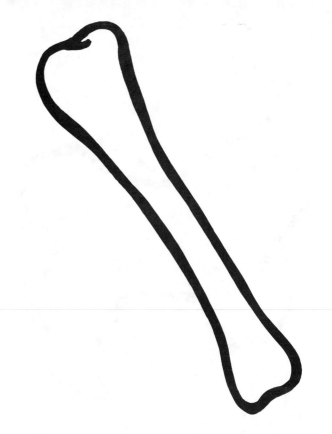

I see a leg bone.

2

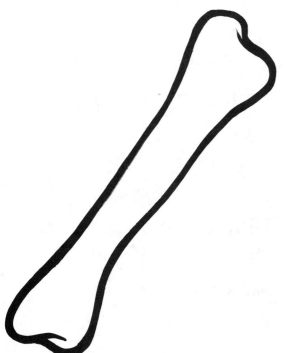

I see an arm bone.

3

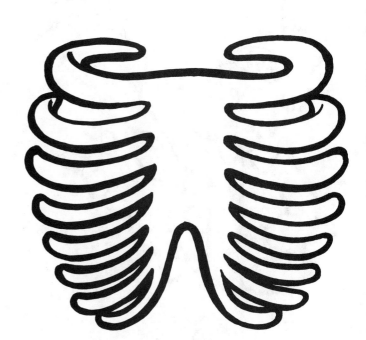

I see a rib bone.

4

35

GA1163

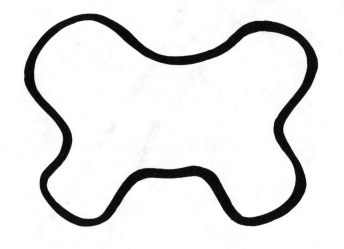

Here is a hipbone.

5

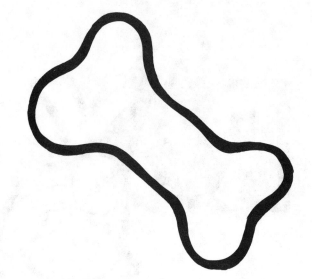

Is that a foot bone?

6

No! It is a dog bone!

7

Directions:
1. Listen to the story.
2. Color the pictures.
3. Cut out the pages.
4. Put the pages in order.
5. Staple the pages.
6. Read the story.
7. Make a cover.

8

36

GA1163

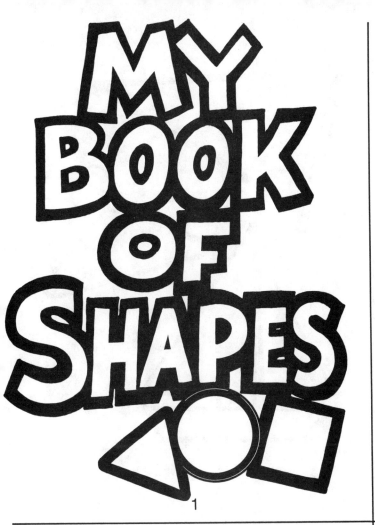

Look all around.
See the shapes.

2

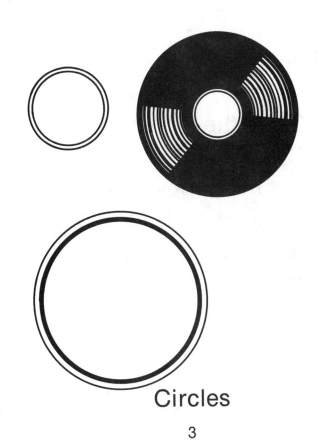

Circles

3

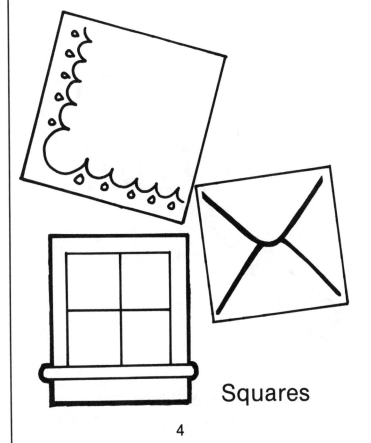

Squares

4

37

Rectangles

5

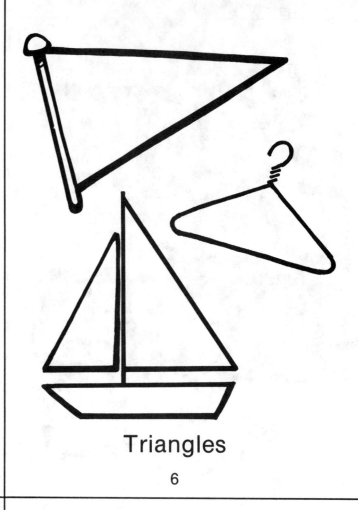

Triangles

6

Ovals

7

Directions:
1. Listen to the story.
2. Color the pictures.
3. Cut out the pages.
4. Put the pages in order.
5. Staple the pages.
6. Read the story.
7. Make a cover.

8

GA1163

1

Jack-o'-lanterns
big and yellow.

2

Witches all in black.

3

Skeletons
run down the street

4

GA1163

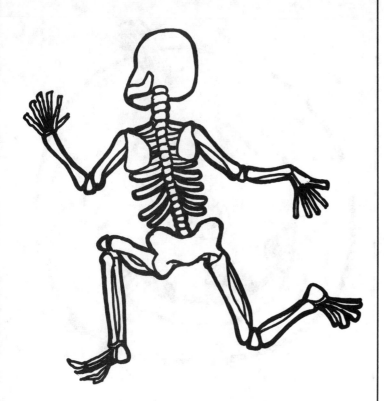

With bones
in front and back.

5

It's Halloween.
It's Halloween.
We all hold out a sack.

6

Trick or treat?
Trick or treat?
Give us something
good to eat.

7

Directions:
1. Listen to the story.
2. Color the pictures.
3. Cut out the pages.
4. Put the pages in order.
5. Staple the pages.
6. Read the story.
7. Make a cover.

8

GA1163

FRUITS

1

Apple

2

Banana

3

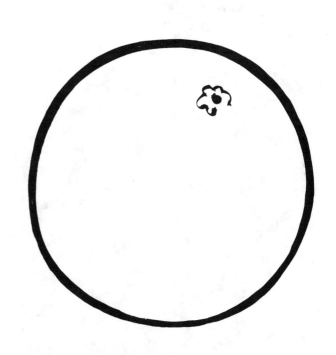

Orange

4

41

GA1163

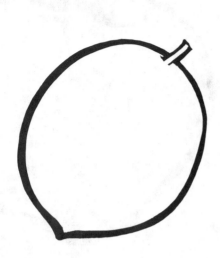

Plum

5

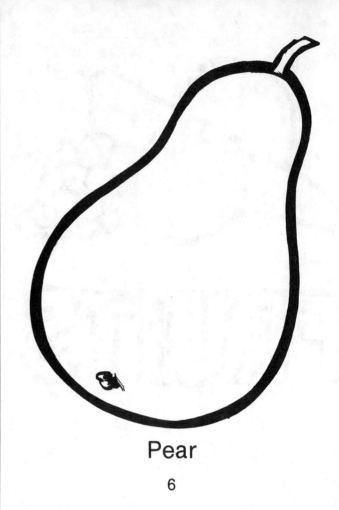

Pear

6

Grapes

7

Directions:
1. Listen to the story.
2. Color the pictures.
3. Cut out the pages.
4. Put the pages in order.
5. Staple the pages.
6. Read the story.
7. Make a cover.

8

42

1

On Monday we ate carrots.

2

On Tuesday we ate corn.

3

On Wednesday we had beans.

4

GA1163

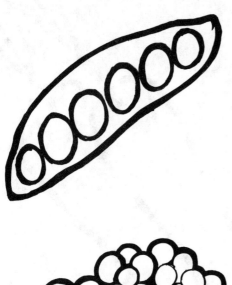

On Thursday we had peas.

5

On Friday I said,
"Mother, please!"

6

"I'm full of veggies
from head to knees!"

7

Directions:
1. Listen to the story.
2. Color the pictures.
3. Cut out the pages.
4. Put the pages in order.
5. Staple the pages.
6. Read the story.
7. Make a cover.

8

GA1163

AN INDIAN STORY

1

Little Bear is an Indian boy.

2

Little Flower is an Indian girl.

3

Little Bear and Little Flower
live in a teepee.

4

45

GA1163

Little Bear and Little Flower
play in the sun.

5

Little Bear rides a pony.

6

Little Flower makes a vase.

7

Directions:
1. Listen to the story.
2. Color the pictures.
3. Cut out the pages.
4. Put the pages in order.
5. Staple the pages.
6. Read the story.
7. Make a cover.

8

46

THANKSGIVING

1

In 1620 the Pilgrims came to America on a ship named the *Mayflower*.

2

They built houses and fences from trees.

3

They planted gardens, hunted wild animals and caught fish.

4

GA1163

They made friends with the Indians. The Indians taught the Pilgrims how to plant corn.

5

The Pilgrims were thankful for good friends, plenty of food and new homes. They had a dinner to celebrate and invited the Indians.

6

Every year in November we have a Thanksgiving dinner with turkey. We give thanks for our blessings, too.

7

Directions:
1. Listen to the story.
2. Color the pictures.
3. Cut out the pages.
4. Put the pages in order.
5. Staple the pages.
6. Read the story.
7. Make a cover.

8

GA1163

MY BOOK OF COLORS

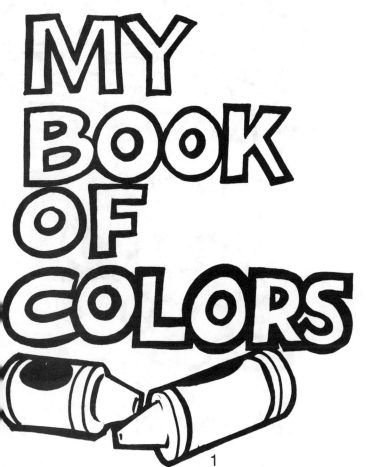

1

What is yellow?

2

What is orange?

3

What is red?

4

GA1163

What is blue?

What is green?

5

What is purple?

6

What is brown?

What is black?

7

Directions:
1. Listen to the story.
2. Color the pictures.
3. Cut out the pages.
4. Put the pages in order.
5. Staple the pages.
6. Read the story.
7. Make a cover.

8

GA1163

MY TEDDY BEAR

1

My teddy bear is
soft and furry.

2

I call him Brownie because
he has brown fur.

3

I can pull Brownie in my
little red wagon.

4

GA1163

Brownie reads books with me.

5

Brownie rides in the car with me.

6

Brownie sleeps with me.

7

Directions:
1. Listen to the story.
2. Color the pictures.
3. Cut out the pages.
4. Put the pages in order.
5. Staple the pages.
6. Read the story.
7. Make a cover.

8

52

1

Outside the weather is cold.
Some days are snowy and icy.

2

Sometimes it is still dark
when we wake up.

3

Animals grow shaggy coats
to keep warm. Some animals
are hibernating.

4

53

We wear hats, coats, boots
and mittens when we go
outside.

5

We play in the snow
and shovel the sidewalk.

6

Inside we sit by the fire and
drink hot chocolate.

7

Directions:
1. Listen to the story.
2. Color the pictures.
3. Cut out the pages.
4. Put the pages in order.
5. Staple the pages.
6. Read the story.
7. Make a cover.

8

GA1163

BUNDLE UP!

1

Put on your hat.

2

Zip up your coat.

3

It's cold outside!

4

55

GA1163

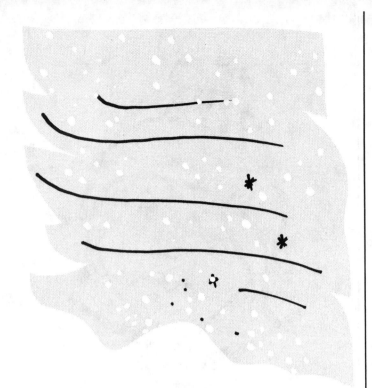

The snow is falling.
The wind is blowing.

5

Put on your boots and
mittens.

6

All bundled up.
Here we go!

7

Directions:
1. Listen to the story.
2. Color the pictures.
3. Cut out the pages.
4. Put the pages in order.
5. Staple the pages.
6. Read the story.
7. Make a cover.

8

CHRISTMAS IS COMING!

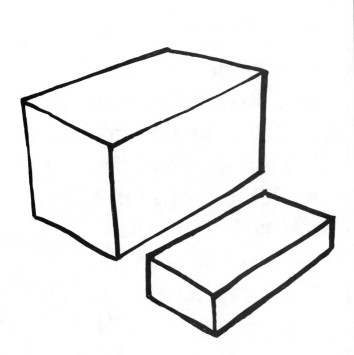

1

Decorate the Christmas tree.

2

Wrap presents.

3

Send cards.

4

GA1163

Bake cookies.

5

Hang a wreath on the door.

6

Sing carols.

7

Directions:
1. Listen to the story.
2. Color the pictures.
3. Cut out the pages.
4. Put the pages in order.
5. Staple the pages.
6. Read the story.
7. Make a cover.

8

GA1163

UNDER THE CHRISTMAS TREE

1

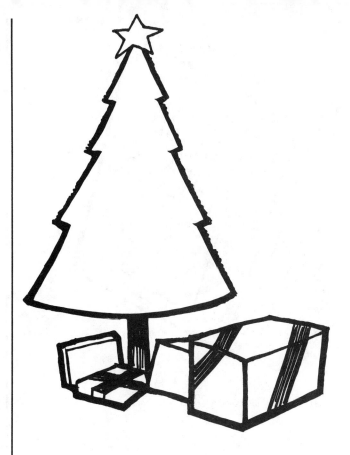

Look at all the presents!

2

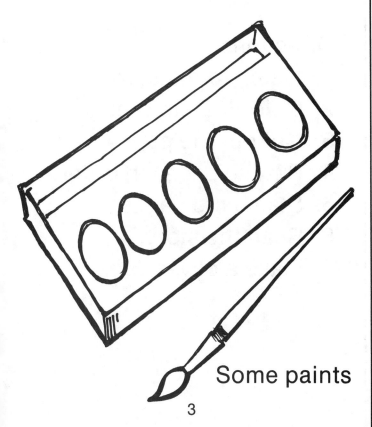

Some paints

3

A bike to ride

4

GA1163

A book

5

A doll

6

A hat and mittens

7

Directions:
1. Listen to the story.
2. Color the pictures.
3. Cut out the pages.
4. Put the pages in order.
5. Staple the pages.
6. Read the story.
7. Make a cover.

8

GA1163

THE THANK-YOU BOOK

1

I say thank you for gifts.

2

I say thank you for helping me.

3

I say thank you for snacks.

4

Mom says thank you for
doing things.

5

Dad says thank you for
doing things.

6

What do you say thank you for?

7

Directions:
1. Listen to the story.
2. Color the pictures.
3. Cut out the pages.
4. Put the pages in order.
5. Staple the pages.
6. Read the story.
7. Make a cover.

8

GA1163

TRACKS IN THE SNOW

1

I see dog tracks in the snow.

2

I see cat tracks in the snow.

3

I see people tracks in the snow.

4

GA1163

I see bird tracks in the snow.

5

I see rabbit tracks in the snow.

6

I see squirrel tracks in the snow.

7

Directions:
1. Listen to the story.
2. Color the pictures.
3. Cut out the pages.
4. Put the pages in order.
5. Staple the pages.
6. Read the story.
7. Make a cover.

8

GA1163

A BIRD FEEDER

1

Find a big milk carton or plastic bottle.

2

Tie a loop to the lid for hanging.

3

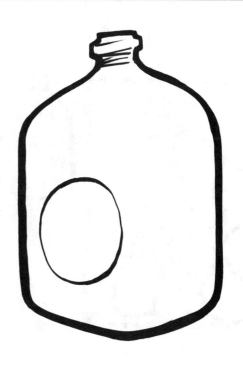

Cut a big window in the side.

4

GA1163

Fill the feeder with birdseed
or bread crumbs.

5

Hang the feeder in a tree.

6

Watch for birds.

7

Directions:
1. Listen to the story.
2. Color the pictures.
3. Cut out the pages.
4. Put the pages in order.
5. Staple the pages.
6. Read the story.
7. Make a cover.

8

GA1163

LET'S MAKE A SNOWMAN

Roll and roll.
Make a big snowball.

1

2

Roll and roll.
Make another snowball.

3

Roll and roll.
Make a funny face.

4

GA1163

Find a hat and scarf.

5

Find a broom.

6

Look!
We made a snowman!

7

Directions:
1. Listen to the story.
2. Color the pictures.
3. Cut out the pages.
4. Put the pages in order.
5. Staple the pages.
6. Read the story.
7. Make a cover.

8

INVENTORY

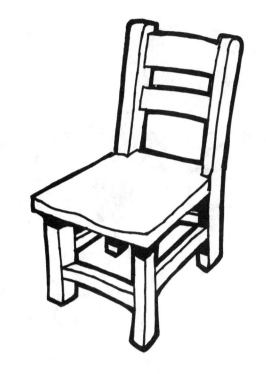

How many chairs? _____

1

2

How many tables? _____

3

How many boys? _____

4

69

How many girls? _____

5

How many pencils? _____

6

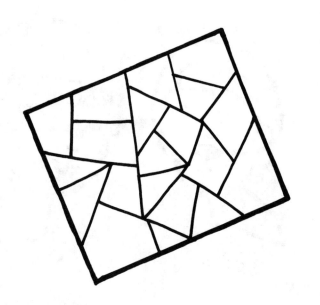

How many puzzles? _____

7

Directions:
1. Listen to the story.
2. Fill in the blanks.
3. Color the pictures.
4. Cut out the pages.
5. Put the pages in order.
6. Staple the pages.
7. Read the story.
8. Make a cover.

8

GA1163

GROUND-HOG

1

Groundhog is sleeping.

2

He wakes up and goes outside.

3

The sun is shining.
Groundhog sees his shadow.

4

GA1163

Groundhog is scared.

5

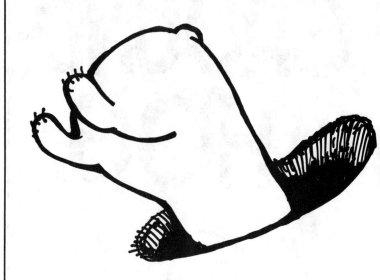

He runs back into his hole.

6

There will be six more
weeks of winter.

7

Directions:
1. Listen to the story.
2. Color the pictures.
3. Cut out the pages.
4. Put the pages in order.
5. Staple the pages.
6. Read the story.
7. Make a cover.

8

BE MY VALENTINE

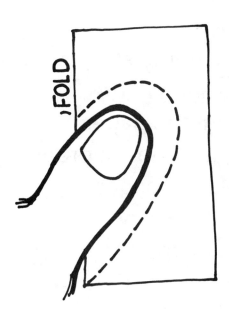

1

Take some red paper.

2

Fold it. Cut around your thumb.

3

Open the paper.
You have a valentine.

4

Write *I love you.*

5

Put on some stickers.

6

Give your valentine
to a friend.

7

Directions:
1. Listen to the story.
2. Color the pictures.
3. Cut out the pages.
4. Put the pages in order.
5. Staple the pages.
6. Read the story.
7. Make a cover.

8

74

PHOTOGRAPHS

1

This is me.

2

Here is my family.

3

Here is my house.

4

GA1163

My family has these pets.

5

My family likes to do this.

6

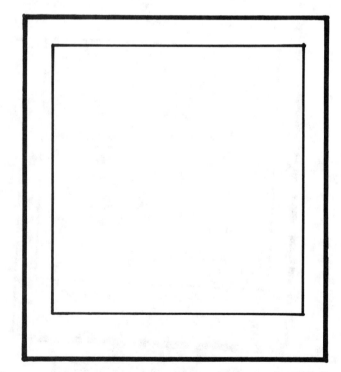

These are our friends.

7

Directions:
1. Listen to the story.
2. Paste on photos.
3. Cut out the pages.
4. Put the pages in order.
5. Staple the pages.
6. Read the story.
7. Make a cover.

8

MY TEETH

1

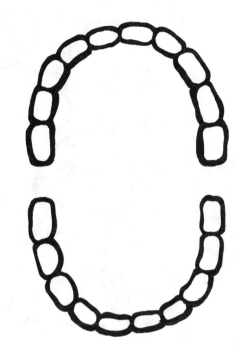

I have twenty primary teeth.

2

I care for my teeth.

3

I brush my teeth after eating.

4

77

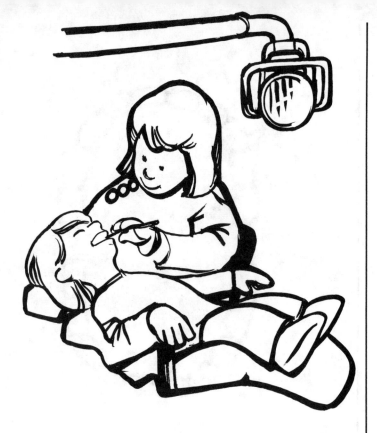

I visit the dentist.

5

I eat the right kinds of food.

6

I want to have a healthy smile.

7

Directions:
1. Listen to the story.
2. Color the pictures.
3. Cut out the pages.
4. Put the pages in order.
5. Staple the pages.
6. Read the story.
7. Make a cover.

8

HATS

1

This is a hat for a fireman.

2

This is a hat for a police officer.

3

A construction worker
wears a hard hat.

4

79

GA1163

A baker wears this hat.

5

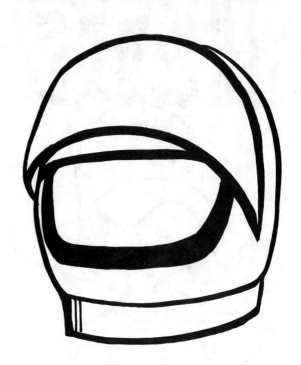

An astronaut wears a space helmet.

6

A cowboy wears this hat.

7

Directions:
1. Listen to the story.
2. Color the pictures.
3. Cut out the pages.
4. Put the pages in order.
5. Staple the pages.
6. Read the story.
7. Make a cover.

8

GA1163

MAKING A PIZZA

1

Pat the dough in
the pizza pan.

2

Spoon the sauce
over the dough.

3

Add the beef or pepperoni.

4

GA1163

Add the cheese.

5

Sprinkle fairy dust on top.

6

Bake the pizza in the oven.

7

Directions:
1. Listen to the story.
2. Color the pictures.
3. Cut out the pages.
4. Put the pages in order.
5. Staple the pages.
6. Read the story.
7. Make a cover.

8

GA1163

MAKING THINGS

1

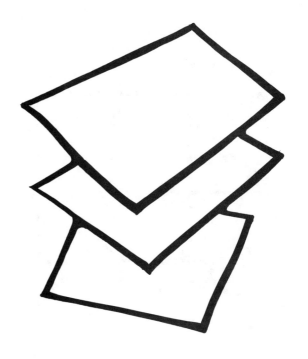

Give me paper.

2

Give me glue.

3

Give me crayons and scissors, too.

4

83

I'll make a truck.

5

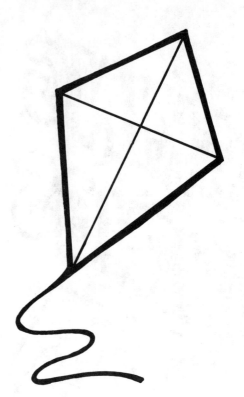

I'll make a kite.

6

I'll make a boat that's
blue and white.

7

Directions:
1. Listen to the story.
2. Color the pictures.
3. Cut out the pages.
4. Put the pages in order.
5. Staple the pages.
6. Read the story.
7. Make a cover.

8

SHOW AND TELL

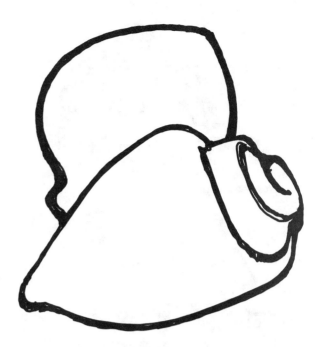

Andy: I got these shells when my family went to Florida.

2

Jack: This is my favorite book. It is about horses.

3

Katy: My aunt gave me this teddy bear. I sleep with it every night.

4

GA1163

Jill: This doll is special.
Her eyes open and close.

5

Chris: I got this soccer ball
for my birthday.

6

Beth: I made this funny hat
from things that I found
around the house.

7

Directions:
1. Listen to the story.
2. Color the pictures.
3. Cut out the pages.
4. Put the pages in order.
5. Staple the pages.
6. Read the story.
7. Make a cover.

8

THE CIRCUS

1

See the little dog climb
the ladder.

2

Look at the clown.
He is so funny.

3

Look! The pretty lady with
the umbrella is walking the
tightrope.

4

GA1163

Look over there! The tiger is
jumping through a hoop of fire.

5

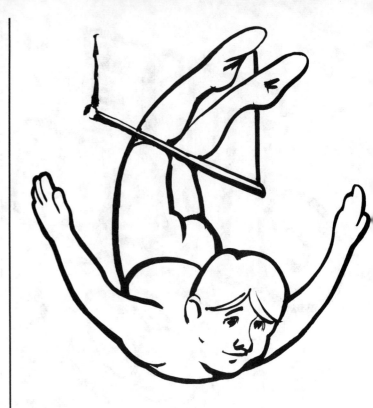

Look up there! See the
acrobat on the flying trapeze.

6

Look! Boys and girls are riding
on the elephant. May I ride, too?

7

Directions:
1. Listen to the story.
2. Color the pictures.
3. Cut out the pages.
4. Put the pages in order.
5. Staple the pages.
6. Read the story.
7. Make a cover.

8

SPRING

1

Let's take a spring walk!

2

The weather is warmer now.

3

Trees have new leaves
and branches.

4

89

Flowers are blooming.

5

Birds are building nests.

6

Smell the fresh air.

7

Directions:
1. Listen to the story.
2. Color the pictures.
3. Cut out the pages.
4. Put the pages in order.
5. Staple the pages.
6. Read the story.
7. Make a cover.

8

GA1163

EASTER

It's time to get our Easter baskets and stuffed bunnies out of the closet.

1

2

We boil eggs and color designs on them.

3

We use a dyeing kit to dye our Easter eggs.

4

We go shopping and buy
some new clothes.

5

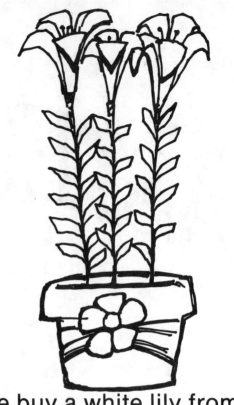

We buy a white lily from
the flower shop.

6

I think about the Easter bunny
coming to my house.

7

Directions:
1. Listen to the story.
2. Color the pictures.
3. Cut out the pages.
4. Put the pages in order.
5. Staple the pages.
6. Read the story.
7. Make a cover.

8

RAIN

1

Rain falls all around,
pitter-patter, pitter-patter.

2

Rain falls on the street.

3

Rain falls on the trees.

4

93

Rain falls on my house.

5

Rain falls on my umbrella.

6

Rain falls all round,
pitter-patter, pitter-patter.

7

Directions:
1. Listen to the story.
2. Color the pictures.
3. Cut out the pages.
4. Put the pages in order.
5. Staple the pages.
6. Read the story.
7. Make a cover.

8

GA1163

GROWING PLANTS

1

You will need—
flower seeds
potting soil
a cup
water

2

Fill a cup with potting soil.

3

Make a few holes in the soil.
Place the seeds in the holes.

4

GA1163

Cover the seeds with a little soil.

5

Water the seeds.

6

Place the cup in the sunlight. Water your seeds when they get dry.

7

Directions:
1. Listen to the story.
2. Color the pictures.
3. Cut out the pages.
4. Put the pages in order.
5. Staple the pages.
6. Read the story.
7. Make a cover.

8

BIRDS

1

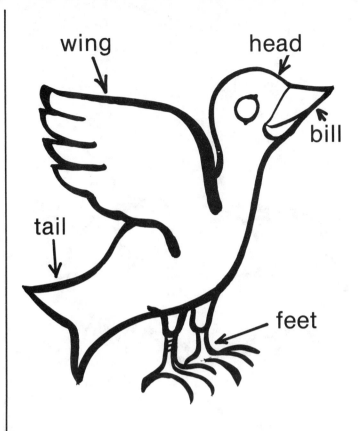

Birds have these body parts.

2

Birds can fly.

3

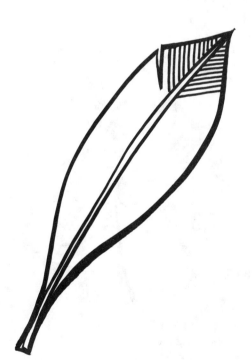

Birds have feathers.

4

97

Birds lay eggs.

5

There are many shapes
and sizes of birds.

6

I can watch birds and listen
to their sounds.

7

Directions:
1. Listen to the story.
2. Color the pictures.
3. Cut out the pages.
4. Put the pages in order.
5. Staple the pages.
6. Read the story.
7. Make a cover.

8

GA1163

GOING CAMPING

1

Jump in the car.
We will go camping.

2

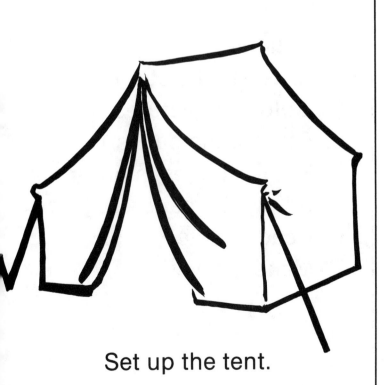

Set up the tent.

3

Make a fire.

4

Roast some hot dogs.

5

Take a walk in the woods.

6

Zip up your sleeping bag.
Good night!

7

Directions:
1. Listen to the story.
2. Color the pictures.
3. Cut out the pages.
4. Put the pages in order.
5. Staple the pages.
6. Read the story.
7. Make a cover.

8

Mother bird needs a nest.

1

2

She will find grass.

She will find mud.

3

4

Mother bird gets twigs.

5

She will get some string, too.

6

She will build a nest for her eggs.

7

Directions:
1. Listen to the story.
2. Color the pictures.
3. Cut out the pages.
4. Put the pages in order.
5. Staple the pages.
6. Read the story.
7. Make a cover.

8

GA1163

BEN BUG

1

Ben Bug is an insect.

2

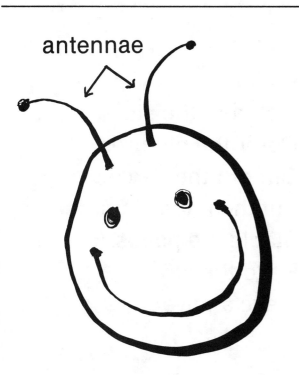

He has two antennae.

3

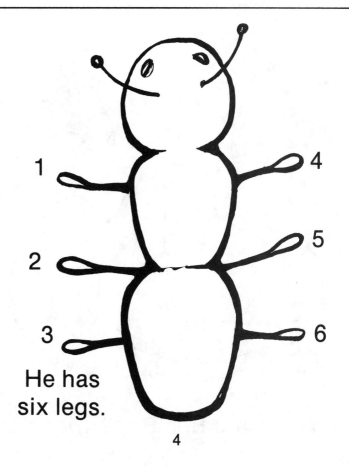

He has six legs.

4

His body is in three sections. He has a head, thorax and abdomen.

5

Ben Bug has holes along the side of his body for breathing.

6

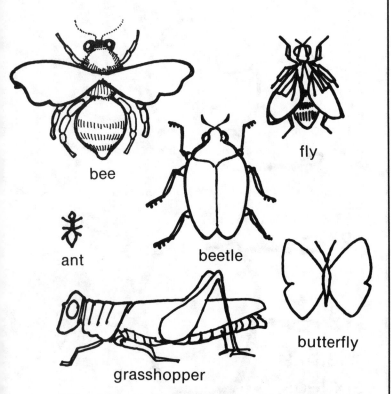

bee

fly

ant

beetle

butterfly

grasshopper

These are Ben Bug's friends.

7

Directions:
1. Listen to the story.
2. Color the pictures.
3. Cut out the pages.
4. Put the pages in order.
5. Staple the pages.
6. Read the story.
7. Make a cover.

8

THE TALL BOOK

A tree is tall.

1

2

A flagpole is tall.

3

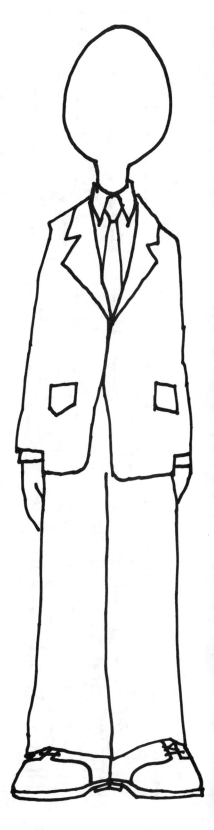

My daddy is tall.

4

GA1163

This building
is tall.

5

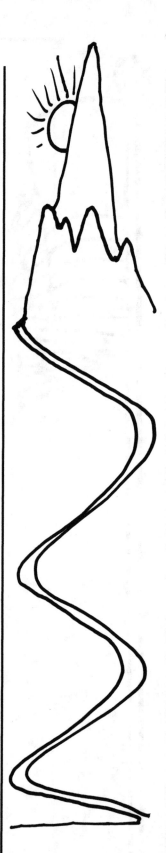

A mountain
is tall.

6

How tall
are you?

7

Directions:
1. Listen
   to the
   story.
2. Color
   the
   pictures.
3. Cut out
   the
   pages.
4. Put the
   pages in
   order.
5. Staple
   the
   pages at
   the top.
6. Read
   the
   story.
7. Make a
   cover.

8

my
mom

1

My mom loves me.

2

My mom cooks.

3

My mom works.

4

My mom tucks me in.

5

My mom dresses me.

6

My mom kisses me.

7

Directions:
1. Listen to the story.
2. Cut out the boxes on pages 1-6.
3. Glue a picture of Mom in the box on page 7.
4. Cut out the pages.
5. Put the pages in order.
6. Staple the pages.
7. Read the story.
8. Make a cover.

8

GA1163

MY
DAD

1

My dad loves me.

2

My dad cooks.

3

My dad works.

4

GA1163

My dad tucks me in.

5

My dad dresses me.

6

My dad kisses me.

7

Directions:
1. Listen to the story.
2. Cut out the boxes on pages 1-6.
3. Glue a picture of Dad in the box on page 7.
4. Cut out the pages.
5. Put the pages in order.
6. Staple the pages.
7. Read the story.
8. Make a cover.

8

GA1163

SEASONS

1

Spring

It is warm and rainy.

2

Summer

It is hot.

3

Fall

It is cool.

4

GA1163

Winter

It is cold and snowy.

5

These are my summer
clothes.

6

These are my winter clothes.

7

Directions:
1. Listen to the story.
2. Color the pictures.
3. Cut out the pages.
4. Put the pages in order.
5. Staple the pages.
6. Read the story.
7. Make a cover.

8

GA1163

FUN IN THE SUN

1

It is a hot day!
Let's go to the beach.

2

We can swim like fish.

3

We can jump over
the waves.

4

GA1163

I can float on my back.

5

We can pick up shells.

6

We can build a sand castle.

7

Directions:
1. Listen to the story.
2. Color the pictures.
3. Cut out the pages.
4. Put the pages in order.
5. Staple the pages.
6. Read the story.
7. Make a cover.

8

GA1163

MY CAT BOOK

1

My cat can sit.

2

My cat can nap.

3

My cat can play.

4

GA1163

My cat can run.

5

My cat can dig.

6

My cat can jump.

7

Directions:
1. Listen to the story.
2. Color the pictures.
3. Cut out the pages.
4. Put the pages in order.
5. Staple the pages.
6. Read the story.
7. Make a cover.

8

PET PARADE

1

Here comes Bill with his dog.

2

Here comes Jan with her cat.

3

Here comes Tim with his fish.

4

117

GA1163

There goes Peg with her bunny.

5

There goes Tom with
his hamster.

6

There goes Bev with her mouse.

7

Directions:
1. Listen to the story.
2. Color the pictures.
3. Cut out the pages.
4. Put the pages in order.
5. Staple the pages.
6. Read the story.
7. Make a cover.

8

118

THE LOST AND FOUND BOX

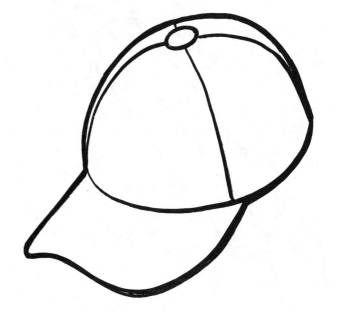

Here is Sam's hat.

2

1

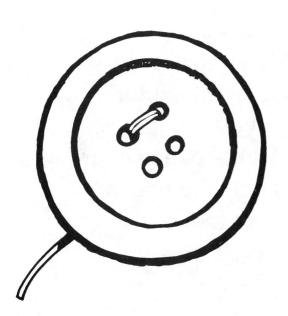

Here is Tim's button.

3

Here is Pam's book.

4

119

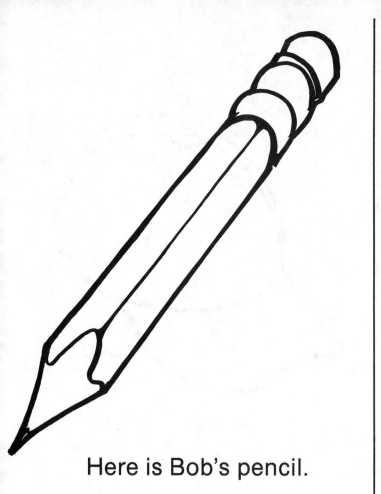

Here is Bob's pencil.

5

Here is Meg's mitten.

6

Here is Kim's coat.

7

Directions:
1. Listen to the story.
2. Color the pictures.
3. Cut out the pages.
4. Put the pages in order.
5. Staple the pages.
6. Read the story.
7. Make a cover.

8

120

GA1163

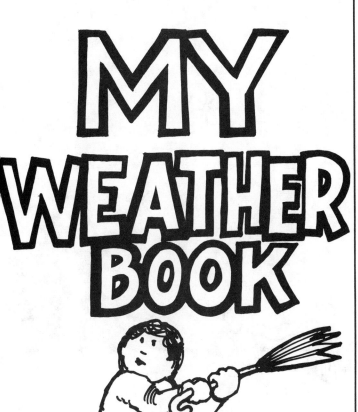

MY WEATHER BOOK

1

It is sunny.

2

It is rainy.

3

It is cloudy.

4

GA1163

It is windy.

5

It is snowy.

6

What is the weather
today? Draw a picture.

7

Directions:
1. Listen to the story.
2. Color the pictures.
3. Cut out the pages.
4. Put the pages in order.
5. Staple the pages.
6. Read the story.
7. Make a cover.

8

GA1163

RHYMES

1

I see a cat on a mat.

2

I see a fox in a box.

3

I see a hen in a pen.

4

GA1163

I see a bug on a jug.

5

I see a bee in a tree.

6

I see a fish in a dish.

7

Directions:
1. Listen to the story.
2. Color the pictures.
3. Cut out the pages.
4. Put the pages in order.
5. Staple the pages.
6. Read the story.
7. Make a cover.

8

I HAVE FEELINGS

1

happy

2

sad

3

mad

4

125

scared

5

excited

6

lonely

7

Directions:
1. Listen to the story.
2. Color the pictures.
3. Cut out the pages.
4. Put the pages in order.
5. Staple the pages.
6. Read the story.
7. Make a cover.

8

GA1163

MY BOOK OF NUMBERS 123

1

1 one

2 two

2

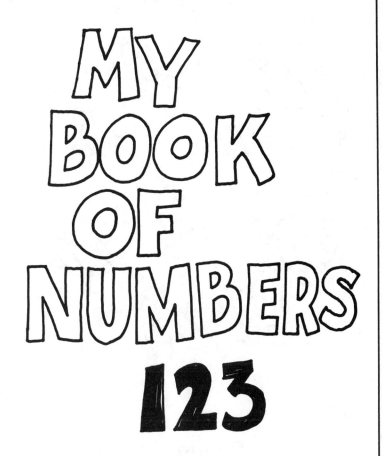

3 three

4 four

3

5 five

6 six

4

7 seven

8 eight

5

9 nine

6

10 ten

7

Directions:
1. Listen to the story.
2. Color the pictures.
3. Cut out the pages.
4. Put the pages in order.
5. Staple the pages.
6. Read the story.
7. Make a cover.

8

THE MAGIC MACHINE

1

Put in a hat.

Out comes a cat!

2

Put in a log.

Out comes a dog!

3

Put in a fan.

Out comes a man!

4

129

GA1163

Put in a pen.

Out comes a hen!

5

Put in a box.

Out comes a fox!

6

Put in a rug.

Out comes a bug!

7

Directions:
1. Listen to the story.
2. Color the pictures.
3. Cut out the pages.
4. Put the pages in order.
5. Staple the pages.
6. Read the story.
7. Make a cover.

8

130

GA1163

THINGS THAT GO

1

A bus can go.

2

A truck can go.

3

A car can go.

4

131

GA1163

A boat can go.

5

A train can go.

6

A plane can go.

7

Directions:
1. Listen to the story.
2. Color the pictures.
3. Cut out the pages.
4. Put the pages in order.
5. Staple the pages.
6. Read the story.
7. Make a cover.

8

GA1163

DINOSAUR STORY

Dinosaurs lived long,
long ago.

1

2

Some dinosaurs
ate plants.

3

Some dinosaurs ate meat.

4

133

A brontosaurus was a very big dinosaur.

5

Tyrannosaurus rex was the king of the dinosaurs.

6

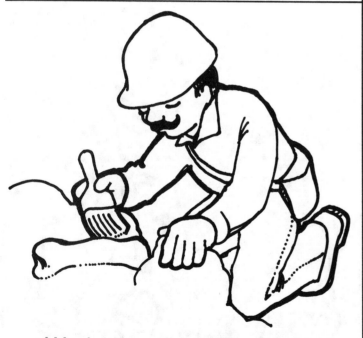

We know about dinosaurs from the fossils we have found.

7

Directions:
1. Listen to the story.
2. Color the pictures.
3. Cut out the pages.
4. Put the pages in order.
5. Staple the pages.
6. Read the story.
7. Make a cover.

8

GA1163

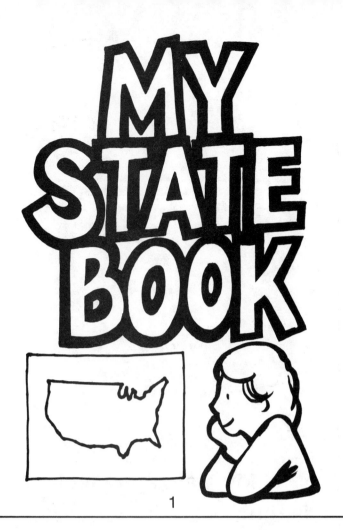

MY STATE BOOK

1

This is the shape
of my state.

2

My state flower is

the _____.

3

My state bird is the

_____.

4

135

GA1163

My state tree is the

_____.

5

My state animal
is the _____.

6

My state song is

_____.

7

Directions:
1. Listen to the story.
2. Draw and color the pictures.
3. Cut out the pages.
4. Put the pages in order.
5. Staple the pages.
6. Read the story.
7. Make a cover.

8

MY BIRTHDAY

1

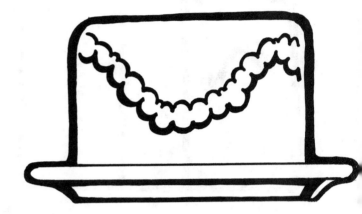

Today is my birthday. I am
_____ years old.

2

My friends will come
to my house for a party.

3

We will play games.

4

GA1163

I will open some presents.

5

We will eat cake and
ice cream.

6

All my friends will
sing "Happy Birthday."

7

Directions:
1. Listen to the story.
2. Fill in the blank.
3. Color the pictures.
4. Cut out the pages.
5. Put the pages in order.
6. Staple the pages.
7. Read the story.
8. Make a cover.

8

THE COLORS OF THE RAINBOW

1

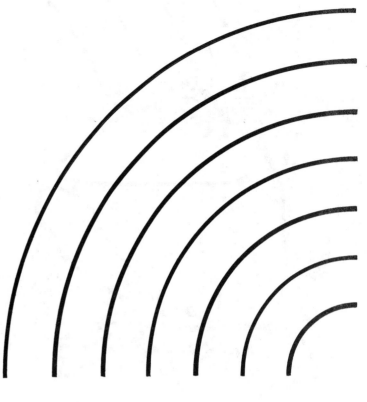

I see red in the rainbow.

2

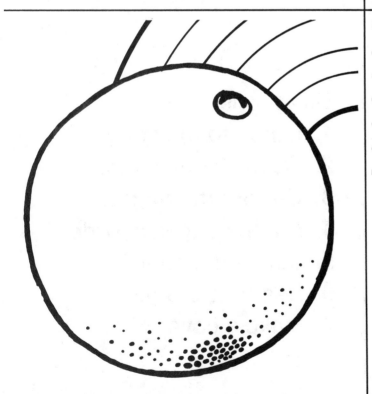

I see orange in the rainbow.

3

I see yellow in the rainbow.

4

139

I see green in the rainbow.

5

I see blue in the rainbow.

6

I see purple in the rainbow.

7

Directions:
1. Listen to the story.
2. Color the pictures.
3. Cut out the pages.
4. Put the pages in order.
5. Staple the pages.
6. Read the story.
7. Make a cover.

8

GA1163